HAUS CURIOSITIES

The Power of Politicians

About the Contributors

Claire Foster-Gilbert is the founder director of the Westminster Abbey Institute. A current and former member of numerous ethics committees, Dr Foster-Gilbert has played an instrumental role in the medical research ethics field, and has led efforts to shift the Church's thinking on environmental issues.

Frances D'Souza is a British scientist and life peer, and was Lord Speaker in the House of Lords between 2011 and 2016. Baroness D'Souza was previously a lecturer at Oxford Brookes University and the London School of Economics, and was director of the human rights charities Article 19 and the Redress Trust.

Tessa Jowell was the Member of Parliament for Dulwich and West Norwood for 23 years. Baroness Jowell also held several major government ministerial and opposition positions, including Secretary of State for Culture, Media and Sport (2001–07) and Minister for the Olympics (2005–10).

Edited and with an Introduction by Claire Foster-Gilbert

THE POWER OF POLITICIANS

A dialogue between Tessa Jowell and Frances D'Souza

First published by Haus Publishing in 2018
4 Cinnamon Row
London SW11 3TW
www.hauspublishing.com

The right of the author to be identified as the author
of this work has been asserted in accordance with
the Copyright, Designs and Patents Act 1988

A CIP catalogue record for this book is
available from the British Library

Print ISBN: 978-1-912208-07-4
Ebook ISBN: 978-1-912208-08-1

Typeset in Garamond by MacGuru Ltd

Printed in Spain

Contents

Acknowledgements

Sincere thanks are due to the Dean and Chapter of Westminster, the Council of Reference and Steering Group of Westminster Abbey Institute, Kathleen James, Barbara Schwepcke, Harry Hall, Ruth Cairns, Seán Moore, Sunbeam House in Hastings and Moore's Cottage in Knockanure, Co Kerry.

Introduction

In 2015 and 2016 Westminster Abbey Institute held a series of dialogues on the subject of power as it is exercised in the institutions of Government, Parliament, the Judiciary and the media. This little book is based upon the dialogue about the power of politicians. By way of introduction I will explain why Westminster Abbey would think it important to host such a dialogue; explore some basic questions about who MPs are, what they are for and how they are perceived; and look at the ways in which Baroness Jowell interpreted her role as she navigated the moral challenges that beset the life of an elected politician.

Just as the editing of this volume was being completed, on 12th May, 2018, Tessa Jowell died of a brain tumour. The courage with which she faced her illness, and the way in which she turned it into a means to serve others, were characteristic. The redoubtable woman who is evident in the words of this dialogue is just the same.

Within the ancient walls of Westminster Abbey, the prayers of those seeking wisdom and forgiveness for themselves and justice and peace for the world have echoed through a thousand years of turbulent history. Whatever else it might have stood for, because it is imbued with centuries of this attentive meditation, Westminster Abbey can and should now offer a place of profound questioning and reflection in the heart of Westminster. Today, the Abbey finds itself on the south side of Parliament Square, with the Houses of Parliament to the east, the Treasury and all of Whitehall to the north and the Supreme Court to the west. It sits at the table, then, with the Legislature, the Executive and the Judiciary: the institutions and people who serve the nation. This geographical privilege belies the fact that the Abbey has little access as of right to the corridors of power. However, when Westminster Abbey Institute was established in 2013 to support the public service of its immediate neighbours, it was welcomed. There was a thirst for depth in the increasingly stretched and stressed body of public servants, like a brittle sponge that needed watering, and the Abbey was acknowledged to be a well that might quench that thirst. Through its Institute, Westminster Abbey tries to bring out into the public domain the rich treasury it has nurtured for so long. Explicitly serving people of all faiths and none, the Institute draws on the Abbey's resources of spirituality and scholarship rooted in its Christian tradition. Out of this deep root comes a disposition to serve the good and the true, and this has forged the Institute's aims: to nurture and revitalise moral and spiritual values in public life; to inspire the vocation to public service in those working in Westminster and Whitehall; to identify and defend what is morally healthy in their institutions; and to promote a wider understanding of public service.

The idea for the programme of dialogues on the nature of power exercised around Parliament Square was partly generated by the play *Protest Song* by Tim Price, which depicts a homeless man politicised by the Occupy movement when it established itself on his patch outside St Paul's Cathedral in 2010–11. The play explores Occupy's notion of power as being entirely in the hands of 1% of the people, while 99% remain victims of the 1%'s imagined unscrupulousness. In the play, the 1% consists of the business and political classes. But the Institute's encounters with those of this so-called 1% working around Parliament Square have revealed human beings who, much of the time, feel anything but powerful. And yet it *is* these people and their institutions who run the country. So, what is the nature of the power of the public servant, and to what end should it be exercised? With these questions in mind we embarked upon a series of dialogues exploring power as a force for good as it is experienced by the people working within the constraints of the UK constitution.

If there is something a politician really believes should be done for the good of the country, how within the ecology of Westminster do they make it happen? Ruling power is located among balancing forces of party politics, Cabinet responsibilities, the Prime Minister's favour, the need to gain and retain votes, the politically impartial support of civil servants, public opinion as it is expressed through traditional and social media and 'events, dear boy, events'. To what extent do the different forces support, curtail, outweigh or even completely scupper each other in the shared attempt to express and enact what should be done for the country? The UK constitution puts elected political leaders at its heart and this is where, rightly, responsibility finally rests for the decisions, called policies, that are brought into being. The volatility that is inherent in democracy – as MPs inevitably have to attend to being selected, elected and re-elected – is then given considerable stabilising ballast by the constitutional provision of a non-political Civil Service, Judiciary, Armed Forces and Security Services and an appointed House of Lords, all of whom, together with MPs themselves, owe loyalty first of all to the Crown, which has no direct power at all. The genius of the system is that no one can become a tyrant, but arguably the very same system prevents anything getting done.

The system of parliamentary democracy within which Tessa Jowell operated, as an MP for 23 years and latterly as a Peer, has evolved over seven centuries, and is still evolving. Parliament consists of two houses, the House of Commons and the House of Lords. The 650 members of the House of Commons, called Members of Parliament, are elected to their places, each representing a constituency. The whole of the UK is divided into these 650 constituencies, so no one is without their MP to represent them, and every adult, with a very few exceptions, is entitled to vote for their MP. Members of the House of Lords (Peers) are appointed, with the exception (somewhat ironically) of 90 hereditary Peers who elect from their own number. Legislation is created in the House of Commons and can be amended by the unelected House of Lords, but it cannot usually be overturned. Nearly all MPs are members of a political party, and the party which gains a majority of MPs in the House of Commons forms Her Majesty's Government, remaining in power until the next election, with the party leader becoming Prime Minister. All the other Ministers who form the Cabinet and run the different Government Departments are chosen by the Prime Minister from among the MPs in their Parliamentary party, and also sometimes from the Lords. Each Government Department (the Home Office; the Treasury; the Department for Environment, Food and Rural Affairs; etc) has one Secretary of State and several junior Ministers. The Secretaries of State meet together regularly as the Cabinet, by whom policies are decided, and they are also known as 'the Front Bench' – that is, they sit on the front benches in the House of Commons' debating Chamber. The political party with the second highest number of MPs forms Her Majesty's Loyal Opposition. MPs in opposition will be appointed to 'shadow' offices, so there will be a Shadow Home Secretary, a Shadow Foreign Secretary, etc. This 'Shadow Cabinet' will sit on the opposition front bench facing the Government front bench in the Chamber.

While Government Ministers will be responsible for creating policies, these have to be debated in Parliament by all MPs. Some of these, of course, are in neither the party that is in power nor that which is in opposition, but Parliament as a whole – all 650 MPs – is responsible for holding the Government to account. The Government is also known as the Executive, as it executes its responsibility to govern the country through the Government Departments. The Government Departments, headed by Ministers who have been democratically elected as MPs, are staffed by civil servants who are not elected but appointed on merit, and are strictly non-political. They must serve their Ministers, whichever political party is in power, bringing Ministers' ideas into carefully drafted policy and then delivering them across the country. The relationship between Minister and civil servant is thus critical to the success of the UK system of Government. Ministers can overwhelm civil servants with too many policy ideas, or with no clarity about policy. Civil servants can stifle the birth of a new policy by being too cautious. Ministers can feel inferior to their civil servants who inevitably know more about the policy area of their Government Department than they do; civil servants can feel overlooked, undervalued and misunderstood if Ministers ignore their advice. Sometimes Ministers go so far as to criticise civil servants in public; this is a cowardly act since civil servants cannot defend themselves in public.

As the dialogue shows, Tessa Jowell was very good at creating teams to make the policies she wanted come into being. For her, civil servants were not an obstacle to but a vital part of good process. But she warned of the danger of policy overload, and counselled identifying a very few policies and seeing them through from announcing them in a speech to their implementation, following through with an audit of their success or otherwise thereafter, never assuming that just making a speech is somehow enough. She learned never to try to implement too many policies, understanding that success depended upon her ability to prioritise. Her relationships with her civil servants were professional, informed by her 20 years of experience of working prior to becoming an MP. Her only complaint, and it was not really a complaint because she understood their need, was about civil servants attempting to control her diary and her time, and ambushing her with paperwork in her ministerial car.

Tessa Jowell presented herself as a public servant in the Gladstone tradition of never allowing private interests to intrude into the public sphere.[1] She could also be said to have sought to exemplify the prayer that is still said every single working day in the Chamber of the House of Commons from the Restoration of Charles II as a constitutional monarch in 1660:

> May they never lead the nation wrongly through love
> of power, desire to please, or unworthy ideals but laying
> aside all private interests and prejudices keep in mind
> their responsibility to seek to improve the condition of
> all mankind.

And yet it is a pervasive and irrational habit, even amongst
the politically engaged and sophisticated, to assert that *all*
politicians present the exact opposite. All politicians are
'corrupt' or at least 'in it for themselves', and are incompetent
at what they do, we lazily comment. Our feelings towards
politicians are ambivalent at best, and we seem to have been
consistently ambivalent, if not downright hostile, through-
out the centuries in which we have enjoyed the privilege of
electing our leaders. Even earlier than Charles II, Shakespeare
had a multitude of insults for politicians, such as Lear's advice
to the blinded Gloucester to 'get thee glass eyes, and like a
scurvy politician seem to see the things thou dost not'.[2] We
laugh knowingly at, and do not challenge, ee cummings' more
recent suggestion that 'a politician is an arse upon which everyone has sat except a man'.[3]

There was no golden age when politicians were univer-
sally liked, admired or believed. Even immediately after the
Second World War, when we might expect a high proportion
of the public to have had trust in politicians, only 40% of us
did. The 'veracity index' published by Ipsos MORI in 2016

had politicians at the bottom of every list of professionals whom we do or don't trust: lower than estate agents and a lot lower than lawyers.[4] (The top five most trusted professionals were doctors, teachers, judges, scientists and hairdressers.)

A confounding, or possibly explanatory, poll was run in 2014 by Ipsos MORI for King's College, London.[5] In that poll, 60% of us thought we expected more of our Government than we do of God. So, on the one hand we don't trust politicians and on the other we expect them to be more trustworthy than the Almighty. We simultaneously believe that they are powerless and that they are all powerful. I would argue that our irrationally extreme contempt for politicians is connected to our equally irrational desire for them to be better than any human can be expected to be. Politicians make promises they and we know they can't keep – but, it seems, we want them to. When in opposition, politicians make sometimes extravagant claims about their ability, were they to be in power, to resolve any number of injustices, to introduce any number of policies that will make all our lives better and to fulfil our hopes and dreams in any number of ways. Then, when they get into power as the elected Government, they find they can do very little of what they promised, and even what they can do is tremendously compromised. As Nick Clegg pointed out in a dialogue at Westminster Abbey Institute in 2017, when in Government, about 90% of what you do is in reaction to events beyond your control.[6] For example, no matter how critical the need, wish or promise for better education, health, housing or employment articulated in May 2017, the Government elected in June 2017 is completely dominated by Brexit, and this would have been the case whichever party had been elected.

We know this to be true, so one might imagine that we would be delighted if a politician came to our door in the lead-up to a General Election and said: 'In all honesty, I'd like to do A, B, C and D when in Government. But if you vote for me, and my party forms the next Government, we're only likely to be able to achieve a bit of B, and maybe some of D in a compromised form. My ambitions are mediocre, but I'm being truthful. We both know events will intervene to undermine anything more successful.' If they did that, we might think we would applaud their honesty and vote for them. On the contrary, it seems we want them to tell us they can give us a better future, come what may. We want them to be our Messiah. 'Corbynmania' was only the latest iteration of this visceral expression of the King's College poll results. We long for someone to sort the mess out, fulfil our dreams. But when they are elected and we find out that their power is relative and that our dreams are not, after all, going to be realised, our mania curdles and turns into hate. There was a phenomenon called 'Cleggmania' in 2010, which swiftly turned once Clegg found himself part of Government and forced to compromise on previously made promises. Without a shadow of a doubt, if Corbyn had won the May 2017 election and become Prime Minister, he would have met with the same callous fate as he struggled to deal with the overwhelming demands of Brexit.

Tessa Jowell confounded this political danger by drawing close to her constituents and staying close to them, no matter how high her political promotion took her. She observed that politicians always start to go wrong when they disconnect themselves from their constituents. As a Minister, she worked out how to deliver effectively just a few promises. And while external events cannot be controlled, she observed, politicians can nevertheless unnecessarily allow one policy to dominate to the detriment of others – as demonstrated by Tony Blair's exclusive attention to the Iraq war.

Democracy requires politicians to be the constant attendants of power. The need to seek and retain power never goes away, and our political leaders are vulnerable to corruption just by virtue of that. Politics is a power game, and it looks like a zero-sum game, insofar as only one person can win a seat in a constituency, only one person can be the Secretary of State in a Government Department, and only one person can be Prime Minister. If I win, you lose, and vice versa. For a democratically elected politician, walking alongside every policy development, every wish for wisdom, is the thought of what its effect will be on gaining or retaining power. It is important to understand and acknowledge that our democracy necessitates this volatility at its heart, or the people would not be able to choose their leaders. It means that democracy obliges a few people, those willing to stand and be counted, to be exposed to the morally corrosive force of power-seeking. And since they are human beings like the rest of us, not the God we want them to be, they are susceptible, and some fall.

Asking how any of us would fare in such an environment is a way of appreciating the position of MPs and their need to arm themselves against this moral corrosion. The atmosphere in the House of Commons can be heady, the stakes high. In no other walk of life can one rise to such dizzy heights of seniority and fame so quickly and on the basis of no apparent merit, nor fall so fast or so far. An MP may be appointed to a ministerial post only in order to achieve a balance in different parts of the Government, or because someone else, whom the Prime Minister did not want to upset, has refused it. They may lose the post because it is politically expedient, as in the 'night of the long knives' of July 2014, one of many examples in history, when a host of Ministers was sacked in order to make way for a more gender-balanced, less politically febrile Cabinet with a better chance in the 2015 elections. However well one may understand the political forces, the giving and withdrawing of power still feels personal – and brutal. Losing is devastating. By the same token winning is intoxicating, and what does the ordinary, fallible human who is not God do with the glorious surge of energy that follows success, surrounded by dependent juniors who are all longing to have a part in their power, to share their glory, to be them one day? What protects against the temptation to abuse that power?

Not independent monitoring bodies. There are five of these, at the last count, with another one threatened in the light of the sex-pest scandal. It is perhaps an indication of the public's realisation that these bodies are not sufficient to ensure good behaviour that the more measures are put in place to guard against corruption and abuse of power, the more public trust decreases, as Lord Bew, Chair of the Committee on Standards in Public Life (till 2018), has observed. There seems to be a direct negative relationship between the two.[7] Tessa Jowell, recognising that we have never trusted politicians, urged us to lower the bar. Instead of the constant disappointment at politicians not being what we think we want them to be, she argued, we have to understand what Parliament is for and what MPs have to do to hold the Executive to account, while at the same time acknowledging that improvements to the institution need to be made.

Rather than depending upon independent bodies to tell her what was the right thing to do, Tessa Jowell attended carefully to her own moral health. Her resistance to the moral perils of political power should give hope to anyone of integrity who is afraid they would only lose their moral compass if they entered political service. In telling her story, drawn out by Baroness D'Souza and audience questions, Tessa Jowell gave a fascinating insight into the workings of Parliament and

Cabinet, the successful development and delivery of policy and the resilience of her interior life. The account is a masterclass in how to be a good politician – good in all senses of the word. It shows how people of goodwill can come to politics and thrive and succeed in this challenging role without loss of integrity. Through the lens of Tessa Jowell's experience and Frances D'Souza's questions the dialogue also attends to deeper questions about what is morally and emotionally demanded of a politician and of the institution of Parliament itself, exposed to the corrosive effects of political power-seeking together with public hostility and indifference. Tessa Jowell's methods for guarding against the corrosive force of political power included building strength through keeping fit and staying close to family and friends, while also maintaining a sense of perspective through two annual disciplines: each year she spent a week of silence at a remote monastery and, in addition, took herself to a place of great deprivation and spent a week with the most vulnerable and needy in society, usually abroad. She worked for many years with a charity in the Dharavi slum in Mumbai, for example. That deep internal reconnection with herself on retreat, and the resetting of priorities enabled by the work with the poorest, gave her great resilience.[8] She sought to mentor junior colleagues rather than bask in their adulation, and she developed those who turned to her into empowered teams engaged together on the causes she championed, such as the London

Olympics of 2012. She also refused to pander to the zero-sum-game myth. She was emphatically not in favour of the antagonistic approach to the weekly Prime Minister's Questions, seeking always instead to win support and cooperation for her policy ideas. Above all, as she herself emphasised, Tessa Jowell was an example of a politician who never lost touch with her true power base, which was her constituents, the real men and women who lived in her neighbourhood and who revitalised her sense of purpose in her work every time she reconnected with them. This enabled her to keep a sense of balance, which seems to be the most important quality for any MP. We could argue that she was protected from the corrosive force of power-seeking because she was in a safe seat, but she kept it safe because she remained always in attendance on her constituents. In so doing, she managed to turn the democratic imperative into a tool for service. In one less attentive to the need to grow and sustain her own resilience, the same imperative could have pandered to her human need for recognition and accolade, and made her morally weak.

We should note that Tessa Jowell's resistance to the intoxicating and morally corrosive effects of power-seeking did not prevent her from being a famous, successful and highly regarded politician. She repeatedly confounded the nasty myths of politics by her insistence on the foundational politics of relationship. She succeeded in retaining the humility of the servant-leader, and she remains an example to those wishing to enter politics, showing how it is possible to succeed without compromising the things that matter. In her conversation with Frances D'Souza, she made a plea for people to seek political office animated by a cause, not by the ability to be selected. And she showed evidence of her own animation in her discussion of mental health in her final answer, perhaps her most powerful statement of all.

Dialogue

Baroness Jowell, speaker in this dialogue, was a Labour Life Peer, elevated to the House of Lords in October 2015 after being in the House of Commons as MP for the constituency of Dulwich and West Norwood from 1992 to 2015. She served as a Minister and Shadow Minister in numerous Departments and was Secretary of State for Culture for many years. Before becoming an MP she trained in psychiatric social work and spent 20 years working in mental health.

Baroness D'Souza, the dialogue's interlocutor, is an independent cross-bench Life Peer sitting in the House of Lords since July 2004. She was Lord Speaker from 2011 to 2017. Her background is in science and she has held academic posts as well as a research consultancy for the United Nations.

Frances D'Souza
Tessa, was there a point in your early life when you thought 'politics is for me'? Did you have a vision of yourself being an MP?

Tessa Jowell
Not as such. Indeed I feel that much of what I have done in my life has been accidental. My first step into politics was

unintended and happened when I was 23. I had allowed my name to go on the ballot paper to be a councillor in the London Borough of Camden because I was promised that there was no chance that I was going to be elected. But then I threw myself into the campaign. I worked very hard for six weeks, I went to every school and I went to every home for elderly people and knocked on every door in this little ward, and I was elected. So I found myself a councillor without ever intending it. There's something of a pattern here. When I went to MIND as assistant director, I actually thought I was applying for a much more junior job and I was slightly overwhelmed when I realised that I was going to be assistant director of the largest mental health charity in the country.

Before politics loomed on my horizon, I trained as a psychiatric social worker. My professional career began in Brixton – later to be part of my constituency – where I was a childcare officer. The second part of my training took place at the Maudsley Hospital. I think I was pretty good as a psychiatric social worker. I did actually manage to help some people to change, people whose lives were in most cases judged to be irredeemably determined by recurrent mental illness.

There's a story from my time in training in Brixton that has influenced my entire political career. It is what moved me from working directly with people to continuing working with people but trying through a campaign organisation – first MIND, then Parliament – to influence the kinds of services they received, and the legislation to which they were subject. This story relates to one particular lady who lived in a block of flats in Brixton. When I encountered her, she had had some sort of collapse of confidence in her ability to relate to people. She had completely withdrawn into herself. Over months, which became years, she never went out, she wouldn't allow anybody in, her electricity and her gas were cut off, food had to be left by the front door and she would take it in and only sometimes would she eat it. She had no bed. In fact, she had no furniture to speak of, and her floor, as in a lot of very poor homes, was lined with newspaper. For six weeks I visited her every week, sometimes twice a week. I would open her letterbox and talk through it to her. After six weeks she invited me in and we spoke together. It was absolutely clear at that stage that she was in a state of acute pain about the way she lived but didn't know how she could change it. I carried on visiting weekly for over three months, sometimes talking through the letterbox, sometimes standing on the threshold, sometimes coming inside, depending on whether she would open the door and then whether she would let me in. And after all those months the great breakthrough came. She agreed with me that we would go and buy her a bed. We went to Bon Marché, a big department store in Brixton. Honestly, I will never forget how I felt walking across the lino floor of the shop with its springy floorboards. The lady was completely dazzled by the noise and the array of things to choose from. I persuaded her to sit on one bed to see if it was comfortable. She did, and then she ordered it. She wasn't short of money. Once she had ordered the bed she began to make a home. She never changed, in that she never became more sociable, but at least she was more comfortable. I eventually left after having worked with her for about 18 months, and I didn't see her again. But her block of flats is in the constituency I represented for 23 years and I think about her every time I drive past it.

I knew there were hundreds of thousands of people like this lady. Through her I learned that change happens in people's lives through a combination of, on the one hand, devoted relationships between people who know each other, and, on the other, the right use of political power to introduce legislation that helps people, to ensure that money flows in the right direction towards effective care for those who most need it, to create different frameworks so that problems are addressed freshly and well, and to enable discrimination to be tackled. And so, for me, politics provided the big solutions, but those solutions had always to be grounded in knowable people's lives. The great power of being a constituency MP is that you can really know the people who live there. Over the years I grew to love the people I represented, and I think they grew to love me too. So, I knew them, but I also had a place at the national political table to try and bring about big solutions.

Frances D'Souza
Aren't you talking about two sorts of power: first, the power of the individual relationship which means really connecting with people and, second, the power of politics? You've had experience of both, but doesn't being in politics inevitably move you away from the former kind of power?

Tessa Jowell
I don't agree that these two sorts of power are separate, or should be separated. I was very engaged with the people that I represented. I think that everything I have ever done has been animated by the faces that I can see. When I stood to be the Labour candidate for Mayor of London, against all expectations, including mine, I didn't win, and the hardest thing for me is that I still carry the faces of the people whose lives I might have been able to change.

Frances D'Souza
It was clearly a traumatic time for you and indeed for many of the people who worked so closely with you for such a long time.

Tessa Jowell
In politics we tend only to talk about our successes, don't we? I've thought a lot about how I coped with that failure and the scale of my disappointment. My disappointment,

which was enormous, was grounded in something which is not sufficiently understood or talked about. This is the unique relationship, responsibility and power that you carry as an elected representative. I knew that I didn't want to continue in the House of Commons and I'm delighted to be in the House of Lords, but I was really excited at the prospect of being the first elected presence in the House of Lords as Mayor of London, representing eight million people. There is nothing like the feeling of responsibility you have when you have been elected, nothing.

You know, the disappointment about not winning affects me deeply, but the thing that really matters is that I tried. I gave it everything I had, intellectually, emotionally, politically and financially. I gave the campaign all the energy I had: I gave it everything. I remain proud of the campaign that I fought. But the reality of politics meant, I realise now, that I could never have won. The Labour Party had changed and in order to be selected as its candidate I would have had to pretend that I had suddenly been reborn as someone of the hard Left. I could never have done that. Even if it had won me a few more votes I would not have been true to myself, and nobody who knew me would have believed it.

Frances D'Souza
Your reflections give rise to an important question in politics, which is about how you manage divided loyalties. You have

said that you never forget your constituents, but surely their needs come into conflict with national needs sometimes? And then there are the different leaders of your party. You served under Tony Blair and Gordon Brown, and you worked with both David and Ed Miliband. These are different politicians with different political leanings. Is your loyalty to the leader, or to the party? And what about your loyalty to your own conscience?

Tessa Jowell
The challenge of working out where my loyalties lay was sharply in focus when I was a Cabinet Minister. As a member of the Cabinet I was bound by collective responsibility. Collective Cabinet responsibility is a doctrine which is also a discipline, binding all of us in the Cabinet. At the extreme, any one of us could experience a point at which they know they cannot support something, and then there is no other option than to resign. But that is an extreme. Collective responsibility as a discipline means you are bound to work hard to find consensus. And, yes, there is also the challenge of being a member of the Parliamentary Labour Party, loyal to the party itself and to its leader, and also a Member of Parliament where you must call Government to account on behalf of the nation's good and the good of your constituents. Within that dynamic I believed that I was bound to be loyal to the person who is the leader of the party. I felt that in relation to Tony

Blair and to Gordon Brown, though it was more difficult with Gordon. I was very close to David Miliband and campaigned for him, but when Ed Miliband was elected leader I became genuinely fond of him. I talked to him a lot, frankly, but always privately. I have had profound disagreements with the two Prime Ministers I've worked for and also Ed Miliband. But I have never made those disagreements public.

Frances D'Souza
Have you ever voted against your conscience?

Tessa Jowell
I haven't, but that doesn't mean that I have easily or lightly voted on troubling issues. My most difficult moment, both as a Member of Parliament and as a member of the Government, was in the run-up to the invasion of Iraq. I recently found the notes that I had made, at the time, of the briefing I received as a Cabinet Minister from the Joint Intelligence Committee and the Security Services. I wrote down what I was told, verbatim. The account that I re-read reflected no doubt at all that Saddam Hussein had weapons of mass destruction, that they could be deployed, that they included a range of chemical and biological agents and that, in being in possession of these, he was clearly in breach of UN resolutions. So, as a member of the Cabinet, I supported the invasion of Iraq as part of the 'coalition of the willing', as it became known.

It was then that I became aware, for the first time and, really, the only time in my experience, that there was a growing gap between my constituents, particularly the faith communities that I represented, and my position in Government. I was deeply disturbed about that. So I called a public meeting in my constituency, which everyone told me was a crazy thing to do. But I wanted people to understand the position that I had taken. I can remember very well driving down Half Moon Lane in Dulwich to the Methodist church hall that evening. The meeting was due to start at eight o'clock. I got there at twenty to eight and already the hall was full. There were 350 people in the hall and about 250 people queuing to get in. It was just me and a local vicar who had agreed to moderate the meeting – no other organisers. It was very ugly and it was very hard to be heard; it was very hard to get my case across. But not only did I hold the meeting, I said to everyone outside that I would hold the same meeting at 10pm if they would like to come back, and I would talk to them then. And that is what I did.

Frances D'Souza
What was the case that you made?

Tessa Jowell
My case was that Saddam Hussein was in breach of UN resolutions, that he had (on the basis of the intelligence that we

had available) chemical and biological agents and that it was very likely, because he had gassed the Kurds, that he would use them again. That was my argument. Everyone shouted and screamed at me in the first meeting. Then almost everybody who had been in the queue outside came back for the second meeting, which, perhaps because it was later, was quieter and less aggressive. In this second meeting, rather – and this is what I found hardest of all – I felt the sense of hurt that people had that I could support this war. They didn't think I was like that, people said to me, and that was really hard to bear. But I stood my ground and I explained many times why I had supported this position. After that the whole mood changed, because people felt that they had been able to own me and my position. It didn't mean that they agreed with me, but they didn't feel this sense of... 'betrayal' might not be quite the right word... doing something that they thought was out of character: not the Tessa Jowell who had represented them for 15 years but somebody else, subject to other forces – because I think what my constituents always felt (I hope they felt) was that their interest was my interest.

So much of what you do and decide in Government is on balance. I was assiduous in my attention to my weekly surgeries. We secured the largest share of money that was going for more primary school places, and we had five secondary schools. My constituents knew that I as their representative could actually deliver things for them, and I was very proud of that. This very precious relationship that I had with them, I felt, faced fracture during the lead-up to the Iraq War. But over time the relationship was rebuilt. I had the most wonderful letters and messages, celebrations and so forth when I stood down. But it was difficult, maintaining the balance between what I took so seriously, the almost sacred responsibility of representation, and my role in Government and in the Cabinet.

Frances D'Souza
It seems clear to me from what you've said that it was your personal connection through being an elected representative with your constituents that actually held your integrity for you and made it impossible for you to go beyond the bounds of your own conscience. So, how did you maintain that connection? For a new MP, the knowledge that he or she is representing a huge number of people, 80,000 or more, is exciting and onerous. It feels an awesome responsibility. But then, after a few years, can it not be that the responsibility becomes more mundane, the surgeries more predictable and routine? Does the allure of power within the party and Government become much more attractive than that of the constituents' needs and the value of spending time with one's constituents?

Tessa Jowell
I never felt that the allure of politics drew me away from my

constituents. For me the difficulty was managing my time, given my different responsibilities. Sometimes, when I was a Cabinet Minister, the sheer logistical challenge of balancing the demands on me felt overwhelming. When you are a Secretary of State, the civil servants in your Government Department want all your time. It is the currency they have to spend. I had the confidence to withstand their demands I think, because I had already had a pretty senior professional life for 20 years before I became an MP. I was used to being clear about what I wanted to get done and how I was going to do it. So I would tell my Private Office that Fridays were for the constituents; I would not undertake ministerial responsibilities on a Friday. I managed to spend about two weekends a month in the constituency even when I was a Secretary of State. There's a sort of game you play with your civil servants. In those days if you were a Minister you would be driven around. This wasn't in order to turn you into a posh woman sitting in the back of a chauffeur-driven car. It was an extension of the sort of indentured slavery the civil servants had you under. They would put a red box on the seat next to you in the back of the car, so that you could sign letters, and they could also put calls through to you, and keep you working. On a Friday, the civil servants would always offer to have me driven to my constituency. I would always refuse and drive myself. There is a point at the bottom of Milkwood Road, where Milkwood Road intersects with Half Moon Lane, on the route I took to get to my constituency. I would reach that point on a Friday and physically breathe more deeply. I knew that I was with my people. It was like being put in my docking station and rebooting. I think that MPs only get into trouble when they become disconnected from their docking station.

Frances D'Souza
So that's your grounding mechanism? Is that what keeps you from the intoxication and even corruption that we know power can bring about? Does it make you resilient? Do you have other things, such as family, yoga?

Tessa Jowell
My constituents were a really important grounding mechanism, and so are my family and my children, my stepchildren, my friends – wonderful friends inside and outside politics. Yoga, yes, the gym very regularly and my little community in my gym.

Frances D'Souza
That's important.

Tessa Jowell
It is. I have one other piece of advice on resilience, to do with time management, and that is to be always where you are not replaceable. In all our lives we feel the conflict of wanting to

do so many things, so the question to ask is whether you could be replaced by someone else who could do it. If you can, then don't do that thing, but instead find and do the thing which only you can do. I had to turn many people's lives upside down a while ago to be with my mother when she died but I would never have been anywhere else. When my son was a little boy and he had the lead in the school play, I suddenly found that I was going to have to introduce a Bill from the Front Bench at the same time as his performance. I had just been promoted and I thought that I would have to resign, because I knew I had to be at my son's play. But Alistair Darling came to the rescue and introduced the Bill for me. The fact is – and this is really important because all of us struggle with it – you can always find someone to help you because they know that you will help them. A number of my colleagues could introduce the Bill, but only I could be at my son's play.

Frances D'Souza

There's a widespread idea, even amongst politically engaged people, that life at the top in politics and the Cabinet is really full of skulduggery and people chivvying for power, and that effectiveness in policymaking is an incidental thing rather than the purpose of high statecraft. You have a reputation for getting your policies through and delivered. What would you advise are the characteristics of effectiveness in getting your policies through?

Tessa Jowell

First of all, you have to be absolutely clear about what it is you want to achieve, and then you have to build a team which has the capacity and capability to achieve that thing. To be effective, you have to understand how change happens, which as I said before includes deep connections between people. So you have to build a team and you have to motivate it: its members have to know that every success is their achievement and every failure is your failure.

Ministers fail for two reasons. First, they try to do too many things and are not clear about what above all they want to achieve. This means that the civil servants in their Department can gain no sense of their priorities and are disempowered. Second, Ministers fail when they think the speech itself is a change. You have a policy idea and you go on the *Today* programme. You announce your idea. Six months later you wonder why nothing has happened. Just saying what you want to do is not enough.

All my earlier professional experience has been useful in my political career, and what I learned as a senior manager and policy analyst taught me the importance of seeing the process right through to delivery and beyond. You start with the speech, which expresses your values and gives a framework for the proposition. You then have to take that framework and set of values and shape them as a policy, a much less exciting but really important stage, and your civil servants are brilliant at this if you harness their skills and experience. With the team that is working with you, you then have to operationalise the policy in whatever way is best to make sure it is carried out – and, again, this might not be exciting or win anyone's attention. It may or may not involve legislation; you have to work out with your team what is the best mode of delivery for the policy. And once the policy is delivered, you and your team must audit it. You have to manage out the unintended consequences that are harmful, and you should also capitalise on the unintended successes. For example: gambling. Gordon Brown emblematically didn't want to support gambling; he didn't want a super casino in Blackpool. It was not legislation that would ever have been top of my list either, but it had to be done. As a result we have the most regulated and the safest gambling industry in the world.

Most importantly you have to understand that political success is not a zero-sum game, however much it may seem that power is in short supply. Politics has a dynamic that can make you think that if the other side wins you have lost, so you have to bring the other side down, which is mad when you think that their 'win' in policy terms could be really good for the country. I've applied everything I learned when I trained to be a psychiatric social worker, especially my clinical training at the Tavistock Clinic in family and marital therapy, to the dynamics of politics and Government. It has helped enormously in confounding the myth of the zero-sum game in politics. The London Olympics was such a success in very large part because we built a team and worked in the way I've described. The team did not consist of egomaniacs but of people who were loyal to each other, loyal to the vision of what this extraordinary thing might do for the country, and were willing and able to see it through to completion. We had to manage delivery very carefully, including not seeking headlines all the time, however tempting. We had to avoid anything that betrayed our efforts and made people feel the Olympics were not theirs. We held the process in trust for the country.

Audience question
Do you think it is better if MPs have had experience of professional life in one form or another before entering politics?

Tessa Jowell
I think that you are a better representative and a more confident one if you have. You can give more to Parliament if you bring actual experience from your earlier life in business, professional life, community activism, whatever it may be. You bring something to Parliament which shapes the passion for why you want to be there. I think otherwise the risk is that people come into Parliament because they are successful at getting selected. Parliament should be full of people who are animated by a sense of cause. I think if you have earlier

experience and a life outside Parliament then you are more likely to be animated in that way. The House of Lords is full of people who bring their outside experience into Parliament, and Parliament is richer as a result.

Audience question

On the television, the House of Commons looks like a room full of people engaged in combative game playing. Are there any reforms you would suggest that would make the House of Commons a better place for running our country?

Tessa Jowell

There is a difference between the showbiz Prime Minister's Questions and other televised parliamentary events and what actually happens.

Some of the very best things I've been involved in as a Member of Parliament, I've done on a cross-party basis. For example, the Olympics would never have worked had I not told the Cabinet that I intended to give the Opposition full briefing on everything to do with the process, including the budget, and did so. I'm greatly in favour of cross-party cooperation and working. It is much easier to do than combative politics. It doesn't need to require you to pretend you're all the same but it means that you can actually establish a working basis on which long-term change can be achieved. One of the causes to which I would have devoted a lot of effort had I become

Mayor of London is the inequality in children's lives, and the prospects that are defined in the first 1,000 days of their lives. Now, there are probably four or five members of the House of Commons and no doubt also members of the House of Lords who have taken that issue, worked together and established a consensus that this is a priority for investment. It won't happen now, but we no longer have to make the case that this is something we have to attend to. In 2015, 40% of the children who started school in London were not ready for school. And they were not ready for school because of the impeded development in their very early childhood. Not being ready for school is the surest indicator of subsequent inequality. And so, I think that if we really want to see long-term change we have to work much harder on how we build those sorts of alliances and coalitions, because there's not much change that is long term and sustained that can be achieved in one term of Parliament.

Audience question
Within a fixed-term Parliament there are plenty of things in domestic and foreign policy that you can start but not finish. Many issues, particularly in longer-term foreign policy, are difficult to deal with. For example, at the moment the radicalisation of some of our youth, our relationships with the Middle East and Russia, are particularly testing. How does the Government, any Government, set the amount of time it is going to devote to long-term strategic aims with particular

reference to foreign policy and our security here and balance those requirements against its need to carry out short-term policies, succeed in those and so be re-elected?

Tessa Jowell

It comes back to an earlier point I made about the importance of focus and being ruthlessly disciplined about the number of issues that are right at the top of the Government's list of priorities. You simply cannot have a Government that is functional and effective if it has 100 priorities. You have to be very, very clear. You also need to be clear that when foreign policies are right at the top of the headlines, news bulletins and everything else, domestic policy is not forgotten. I think there are many ways in which Tony Blair was damaged by the Iraq war, and one was the sense that having been the Prime Minister who started with the promise of a really different kind of Government, he had become distracted by this major foreign policy question. I can remember sitting with a group of single mums in the south of my constituency and one of them said: 'It's just like my husband. I had a husband and he effed off with someone else, just as Tony Blair's effed off to Iraq'. It can be a distraction and it is very important to guard against it. Foreign policy is so critical because the first obligation of Government is to keep its people safe. That is where foreign policy and domestic policy really come together. Radicalisation is a huge challenge that requires long-term commitment, not just thinking about the 15- and 16-year-olds now, but the little ones that are starting nursery schools, building in them a sense of confidence that they belong in our community, that they are proud of their identity as British citizens and that they have hope – because radicalisation is a response to hopelessness.

Audience question

When you were a backbencher, did you have the feeling that the procedural framework within which you had to operate frustrated or facilitated your ability to get things done, and did your perspective on that change at all in Government?

Tessa Jowell

I was never as adept at using procedure in creative ways as some of my colleagues. There are Parliamentarians, and I think of someone like Frank Field MP, who will tend to be non-tribally passionate about particular causes, who become masters of procedure. The problem is that what they are doing is only understood by a very small number of people who are actually physically in the Chamber, so it's not the stuff of great heroics that command the headlines the next day. But just as it is important to know how a car works when you get into it, in the same way if you hold a position in the House of Commons or the House of Lords you have to know how they work. You have to know how they work in order to utilise every opportunity that they can avail. That includes getting people to help you to achieve what you want. I mentored a lot of new MPs. Prime Minister's Questions is the first big moment of opportunity for a new MP. One of my mentees would contact me and say something like 'I've got question number three on PMQs; can you help me?' I would ask them, 'What is it you want to get from this?' Because if you're a new Labour MP (in opposition) you might want to play 'poke the PM in the eye, make him squirm'. That is enticing, but very hard to do. All the power in every sense is with the PM. They have been thoroughly briefed, know all about you and have the backbenchers shouting at you if you're rude. The more important thing for you as a new MP is that you want a story in your local paper about the issue you've raised for your constituents. Even better if you can get the PM to agree to meet you, or if they commend what you are doing. It's quite different from promoting the adversarial approach. I tried to avoid point-scoring myself, and I didn't always get it right, but sometimes people said to me, 'everybody falls quiet when you stand up because they want to listen to what you have to say'. I never used to poke the PM or anyone else on the opposite benches in the eye, but I used to make good progress on the issues I was working on. In 2014 I was engaged in a big campaign on transfer tax and how much commission people have to pay if they're sending money home to a developing country. It was very important that the PM agreed to support my efforts. I needed his agreement to support the work I was leading on early childhood development, and also on the UN's Sustainable Development Goals. There are many MPs who have the same success, but it means stepping out of the 'spit in his eye and make him squirm' dynamic.

Audience question

I want to ask you about the institutional side of power. You've been very clear about the effects and impact you can have personally in exercising power as an MP, but what about the institution of Parliament itself? It can exercise power, but only by winning the trust and respect of the public. In a society that is becoming increasingly demanding and cynical, it seems to me that the degree to which Parliament as an institution can command that respect is becoming hugely diminished. And if that is the case, isn't our system of Government much less able to flourish and to be effective? Are you concerned about the public's attitude to Parliament and whether it is eroding the ability of Parliament to exercise the power that ought to be exercised in a democracy of our kind?

Tessa Jowell

I feel I have only half an answer to your question about power and the competence of Parliament. I think that for Governments with small majorities there has to be a will to collaborate on critical issues such as whether or not to authorise military action in Syria or to undertake substantial welfare reform. These can only be done with cross-party consent. I think that is what the country wants. Parliament *is* powerful. It is disturbing that MPs are not trusted, but instead of talking about restoring trust in politics we need to find a different language. Trust is just too high a bar and although levels of public trust are lower than before, they are not dramatically lower, even though there is so much talk of the collapse of trust. So, I think that we have to start thinking about it in a different way, in a way which recognises the fundamental purpose of Parliament, which is to hold the Executive to account. But changes are needed. We need to select and elect MPs who bring experience of the world outside Parliament to their role, not just a limited experience of politics. Five years is too long for a fixed-term Parliament. All the parties need to undertake a real commitment to promoting more diversity. We should lower the voting age. These are some of the ways in which our Parliament can become more representative and more useful.

Audience question

The Labour Government (of 1997–2010) changed the contracts of GPs to the advantage of GPs. Now these GPs are very reluctant to relinquish the advantages that were given to them. What is your view on this? Do you think the doctors will go on strike? Do you think they should go on strike? Do you think they still have a sense of vocation in this country?

Tessa Jowell

Not for one moment do I doubt the vocation of doctors, but I hope they don't go on strike. The contract that we agreed while we were in Government, which has been heavily misrepresented in subsequent reporting, was part of an investment in the NHS, the result of which meant that when we left power in 2010, recorded satisfaction with the NHS was at its highest-ever level. What people cherished more than anything else in their approval of the NHS was the kindness of nurses (and for that read also doctors and junior doctors). This underlines the point I have been making all along, that it is human relationships that make things work. I absolutely will not join in the trashing of junior doctors. I hope that they and the Government come back from the brink of a breakdown in talks, because strike action is not going to help people who need their care.

Audience question

I want to ask whether you feel power in this country has been vested in the wrong people or the wrong institution at any time during your career.

Tessa Jowell

That has got to be the case. In a way the question then is, what do you about it? The failure to regulate the banking industry has now been very well documented. But institutions and power structures have to respect the dynamism of change. A banking system which has to deal with the scale of globalisation is different from the kind of banking system where everyone writes out their cheques, goes into their local banks to pay them and keeps their savings in ISAs and Premium Bonds. Big institutions need to be able to adapt and change. But the values of public service identified by Lord Nolan in 1995, of selflessness, integrity, objectivity, accountability, openness, honesty and leadership, remain fundamental whatever changes, and apply to all sectors, not just those formally defined as public service.

Audience question

Would you comment on the mental health of this country?

Tessa Jowell

I no longer have a role with MIND, but I am very aware of mental health still. I think mental illness is the hidden and unspoken crisis in our country. People young and old are afraid to talk about it. It is overwhelming in all sorts of proxy ways, including in community and GP services. There is, I think, a yawning gap between the role of psychiatric units and the quality and levels of support in the community. When I was a psychiatric social worker at the Maudsley, with others I undertook a study on what it is about apparently similar social circumstances that lead to dramatically different outcomes. Why do some people manage when they leave hospital after a long period in a psychiatric unit and why do other people fail? Our study identified that it is essentially down to the number of people with whom you are in regular contact. This is really the politics of relationships that we touched on earlier. Over the length of this study we showed that if you are mentally fragile and are not regularly in touch with at least four people, it is very hard to cope in the community.

I think mental illness is a major issue. Since we know that some of the healing and support for mental illness comes from communities, more resources and capacity to support should go to local neighbourhoods. But I also think that we have to outlaw discrimination. Even politically sophisticated people have a woeful ignorance of the hurt they can cause by stigmatising mental illness. For example, Ken Livingstone was outrageous in his recent response to Kevan Jones MP. Kevan had previously spoken about his depression very bravely in a debate in the Chamber. When, more recently, he criticised Ken Livingstone's appointment by Jeremy Corbyn to a defence review, Ken's response was to suggest that Kevan was depressed again and should go and see his GP. It was a disgraceful thing to say. It's an example of how even the political sophistication of Ken Livingstone doesn't act as a barrier to insulting people who have a history of mental illness.

Frances D'Souza
Thank you very much, Tessa Jowell.

Who could have known that this interview would be among Tessa's last public words? All of us involved in organising this dialogue are profoundly grateful to have had such an insight into Tessa's thoughts, career and commitment. We mark this occasion as the beginning of a move towards decent, compassionate and effective politics and politicians.

Notes

1   Claire Foster-Gilbert (ed.), *The Moral Heart of Public Service* (London, JKP, 2014), p. 61.

2   William Shakespeare, *King Lear* (London, Penguin, 2005), Act IV scene 6.

3   ee cummings, "A Politician", *One Times One* (New York, Liveright, 2002), p. 10.

4   Bobby Duffy and Michael Clemence, *Veracity Index 2015* (London, Ipsos MORI, 2016).

5   Ipsos MORI, *Ipsos MORI Leader Perceptions Poll* (London, Ipsos MORI, 2014).

6   Nick Clegg, *The Coarsening of Political Language*, dialogue with Mark Easton, Westminster Abbey Institute, 13th November 2017.

7   Personal communication, 2016.

8   Personal communication, 2015.

Westminster Abbey Institute

The Power of Politicians is published in partnership with Westminster Abbey Institute. Westminster Abbey Institute was established in 2013 to nurture and revitalise moral and spiritual values in public life, inspire the vocation to public service in those working in Westminster and Whitehall, identify and defend what is morally healthy in their institutions and promote wider understanding of public service. The Institute draws on Westminster Abbey's resources of spirituality and scholarship, rooted in its Christian tradition and long history as a place of quiet reflection on Parliament Square.

ALSO IN THIS SERIES

The Power of Civil Servants
The Power of Journalists
The Power of Judges